SWEET TALKS WITH

GOD

Sweet Talks with

GOD

Evelyn Geisler

Pleasant Word

A Division of WINEPRESS PUBLISHING

Pleasant Word (a division of WinePress Publishing, PO Box 428, Enumclaw, WA 98022) functions only as book publisher. As such, the ultimate design, content, editorial accuracy, and views expressed or implied in this work are those of the author.

Unless otherwise noted, all Scriptures are taken from the *Holy Bible, New International Version®, NIV®*. Copyright © 1973, 1978, 1984 by the International Bible Society. Used by permission of Zondervan. All rights reserved.

Scripture references marked KJV are taken from the King James Version of the Bible.

Scripture references marked NASB are taken from the New American Standard Bible, © 1960, 1963, 1968, 1971, 1972, 1973, 1975, 1977 by The Lockman Foundation. Used by permission.

ISBN 13: 978-1-4141-1213-8
ISBN 10: 1-4141-1213-0
Library of Congress Catalog Card Number: 2008902642

CONTENTS

DIAGNOSIS

SWEET TALK 1

When you pass through the waters, I will be with you; and when you pass through the rivers, they will not sweep over you. When you walk through the fire, you will not be burned; the flames will not set you ablaze. For I am the LORD, your God, the Holy One of Israel, your Savior...

—Isa. 43:2-3 NIV

I have diabetes. I don't understand, Lord. Yesterday I was fine, but today I have a disease.

The doctor's lips keep moving after he tells me, but all I can hear are the questions swirling in my head. Will I be able to do the things I want to do? Will I be able to eat the food I want to eat? Will I have problems with diabetes? I have so many questions, but no answers.

After I leave the doctor's office, I sit in the car, feeling like the air has been sucked out of me. Lord, you know I'm overwhelmed. I take a few deep breaths and pray to you for strength and guidance. You answer by giving me that peace that passes all understanding, and I feel myself relax.

I don't know what's ahead for me, Lord, but I trust you. I know you will be with me. I need your strength and guidance to endure this trial.

I start the car and head home. It's time to tell the family.

Prayer: Lord, I don't know what lies ahead, but I do know that you cause all things to work together for the good of those who love you. Please guide me and give me the knowledge I need. Amen.

Sweet Talk 2

Train a child in the way he should go, and when he is old he will not turn from it.

—Prov. 22:6 NIV

Praise be to the LORD, to God our Savior, who daily bears our burdens.

—Ps. 68:19 NIV

My child has diabetes. It came on so suddenly. One day he was a healthy, active youngster—the next day a very sick child in the hospital with an IV running in his arm. We sat and held his hand as the doctor gave us the diagnosis.

After the shock passed, my wife and I plunged in and took the classes the hospital offered and read everything we could to help our youngster. We cried when he cried at the needle pokes and finger sticks.

We hugged him and told him we loved him when he needed comforting. We started teaching him the things he needed to know to take care of his own diabetes.

Now he's getting older and becoming more responsible. We are so proud to see him taking charge of his diabetes. Still, Lord, I don't sleep. I worry that he'll go low in the middle of the night. I'm afraid he'll exercise too much at school without enough to eat or that he'll make the wrong food choices.

I'm frustrated because I can't always be with him to watch over him. I worry, too, that I'm not giving enough attention to our other children. But I know you are everywhere, Lord, and you can do all things. You will help me bear this burden.

Prayer: Dear Lord, please give me the strength and wisdom to care for everyone in my family. Remind me that you are the all-caring, almighty God who hears our cry. Amen.

EDUCATION

Sweet Talk 3

I will guide you in the way of wisdom and lead you along the straight paths.

—Prov. 4:11 NIV

So much to learn. My husband and I went to our first class today to find out about diabetes. We met some other nice folks there—all of us struggling to learn about the disease and how to deal with it. We were glad to be with other people who were in the same boat. From what the teacher said, that boat is pretty large. Many people in this country have diabetes.

The instructor was nice. She said we'd learn about lots of things like medicines, exercise, diet, how to measure blood sugar, and what can happen if blood sugar isn't kept under control. I'm glad there are people like her who can help us sort out what we can do to manage diabetes. I'm glad you're there, too, Lord to guide us all—teacher and students—so that we may receive the tools we need to make diabetes fit into our lives.

I'm going to take careful notes in each class so I can help my husband with his diabetes. I need to know as much about it as he does, so that we can work as a team to cope with this disease.

Prayer: I know we have another team member, Lord. You're our captain, and I pray that you will give us the wisdom and strength to deal with diabetes. Amen.

SWEET TALK 4

For the word of the cross is folly to those who are perishing, but to us who are being saved it is the power of God.

—1 Cor. 1:18 NASB

It was like I'd never seen a can of chili before. Because I have diabetes, now I have to read labels to know how many carbs, fats, and proteins each item contains. The first time I grocery-shopped after being diagnosed, it took me two-and-a-half hours to figure out what to buy.

Luckily the education class helped me sort out what the label was trying to tell me. I learned there are different types of fats and carbohydrates. I also learned what those little initials "g" and "mg" meant.

Shopping for food isn't so daunting now that I've found good quality brands and know what I'm looking for on a food label.

Just as food labels were once a mystery for me, so was the Word of God. As I was growing up, I needed the guidance of my parents, the Sunday school teacher, and the pastor to figure out what God was trying to tell me through His Word.

I will continue to study both God's Word and diabetes throughout the rest of my life so that I may be healthy in both body and soul.

Prayer: Lord, thank you for the opportunity to learn and grow. Thank you for sending people who are willing to share their knowledge and wisdom to help me learn. Amen.

CHALLENGES

Sweet Talk 5

No temptation has seized you except what is common to man. And God is faithful; he will not let you be tempted beyond what you can bear. But when you are tempted, he will also provide a way out so that you can stand up under it.
                    —1 Cor. 10:13 NIV

Lord, I know you promise not to send any more trials than we can bear, but I got pretty close to that line today. The diabetes police were out in force. I went to a party, and my relatives were all over me about what I should and shouldn't eat. I know they mean well, but I don't enjoy being treated like a small child. Instead of enjoying myself, I got angry with those who love me.

How am I going to handle this problem? I want to see my relatives, but I don't want them hovering over me. How can I reach them and not hurt their feelings?

Maybe the best thing to do is invite them over for an informal diabetes class. My family and I can explain how we figure out what we're going to eat every day. I can also tell them about my exercise plan, and encourage them to exercise, too. After all, living with diabetes means living a healthy lifestyle. Then I can treat them to a fine party with good, healthy snacks.

I'll set up a Diabetes 101 class and then call them tomorrow.

Prayer: Thank you, Lord, for listening to my problem and providing an answer. You truly provide a way out of all trials. Amen.

SWEET TALK 6

*He provides food for those who fear him; he
remembers his covenant forever.*

—Ps. 111:5 NIV

*My help comes from the LORD, the Maker of heaven
and earth.*

—Ps. 121:2 NIV

What am I allowed to eat? The question nagged
at me as I searched through my pantry. Foods
like canned fruit that seemed harmless yesterday
posed a threat today because they contained sugar.
Were they the enemy now?

The names of popular diets also flitted in and
out of my head while I looked at food labels. What
should I do? Count calories, figure out fat grams,
play with the glycemic index or go low-carb?

Planning a menu had suddenly become so overwhelming that it seemed easier to eat nothing at all, but I knew that was dangerous too. I called my doctor and got a referral to a dietitian. She helped me fit the foods I liked into a meal plan that I could follow.

I realized then that there are lots of helpers for me to call on if I need them—pharmacists, dietitians, exercise experts, doctors, and many others. But there is one Helper who is above all, and who directs me as I work through my problems. His hand is always ready to guide me. He is the Lord God.

Prayer: Thank you, Lord, for providing me with the wisdom to seek help. Thank you also for providing people who are eager to help me and others like me to work out solutions to living with diabetes. Thank you for always being with me. Amen.

Sweet Talk 7

For I am the LORD, your God, who takes hold of your right hand and says to you, Do not fear; I will help you.

—Isa. 41:13 NIV

I felt like throwing the monitor across the floor. Another reading over 200. I'd been told to think of my blood sugar readings as points of information, but it was getting tough. Testing wasn't much fun either. My fingers were getting sore. Why do it anyway if all I was getting were high readings? I was eating right, sticking to my exercise plan, and taking my medicine on time. What more could I do?

I put the monitor in the closet for a few days. I just couldn't take seeing another "200" flash on the screen. Then one day I had to take a long motor trip.

I thought of the consequences of going low while driving, so I got the monitor out and tested. I was in a safe range, and the trip went fine. I made up my mind to call my educator when I got back to find out why I was running high.

After looking at my readings, my educator went over everything I was doing, then asked whether I had any stress in my life. Of course! I had a tight deadline on a new project at work. My body had been trying to tell me something, and I didn't listen. Both high and low readings are truly instructional.

I also found out that the Lord is truly there to take my right hand. Please do it gently though, Lord. My hand's a little sore from the finger sticks.

Prayer: Thank you, Lord, for reminding me that all aspects of diabetes care are important and that I can learn something new about diabetes every day. Amen.

Sweet Talk 8

*For this God is our God for ever and ever; he will
be our guide even to the end.*

—Ps. 48:14 NIV

Record, record, record. That's all I've been doing
all day. I've taken my blood sugars before and
after meals. I've written down everything I've eaten
and totaled up my exercise. I've entered the unusual
circumstances that occurred during the day, like eating that sliver of birthday cake because I didn't want
to hurt my co-worker's feelings. I've got a lot of facts
and figures, but how do I sort them all out?

I started by highlighting high readings and cir-
cling low readings in red as my educator suggested.
Patterns started to emerge. Seems I always ran low
about 10:30 a.m. Maybe I should add a snack about

10:00 a.m. I always ran high before dinner, too. Maybe I'm eating too many carbs at lunch.

My doctor and educator say they need all this data to help me manage my diabetes, but it sure takes time—time that I'd like to spend doing other things. But how could I better spend my time? The few minutes it takes to record things are buying me more time with my family as I learn to better manage diabetes. Just as you, Lord, are my Guide through all my life, these numbers are my guide through diabetes.

Prayer: Lord, please help me to realize that you are my Helper and Guide through this maze of diabetes. Help me to realize also that I have many tools to call on to lead a healthy life. And just as there are patterns in diabetes, Lord, let me keep you in the pattern of my life. Amen.

SWEET TALK 9

Commit to the LORD *whatever you do, and your plans will succeed.*
—Prov. 16:3 NIV

What a mess! My bedroom looks like the scene of some natural disaster—clothes and supplies are strewn everywhere. I'm traveling to a place I've never been before, and I want to make sure I don't forget to take anything.

Out comes the bag I put all my diabetes supplies in. I slip in the monitor, strips, and sugar tablets. The syringes and ketone test strips go in next. I decide to pack the insulin later when it's closer to time to leave. Got to make sure the insulin has a pharmacy label on it in case the folks at the airport have any questions. Probably should pack a snack, too, just in case the plane is delayed.

So many things to remember. What if I forget something? I sit on the bed, trying to think of every possible thing I might need. I jump up and stuff more items in my suitcase.

Then I feel your comforting arm around me, Lord. I know you are with me, and you'll watch over me on this trip. If anything unforeseen happens, I know you will be there to help me, just as you help me through the trip called life.

Prayer: Lord, thank you for your constant presence in my life, for your watchfulness, and for your loving care. Amen.

Sweet Talk 10

You have made known to me the path of life; you will fill me with joy in your presence, with eternal pleasures at your right hand.

—Ps. 16:11 NIV

I promised myself when I went to my niece's wedding, I wouldn't overdo it at the reception. But I did. All the food looked so good—the rolls, the wedding cake, the ice cream.

Carb counting went the way of the bride's tossed bouquet as I heaped food onto my plate. While my family and I chatted, I kept spooning treats into my mouth. After the bride and groom sped off under a shower of rice, I realized I had no idea how much I'd eaten. But my monitor knew. The reading was high. Talk about wake-up calls.

I thought back over the last few weeks. I'd been letting my exercise schedule slide, promising myself I'd make up for it on the weekends. I'd eaten too many carbs at one meal, assuring myself that I'd eat lighter at the next one. Several times I'd forgotten to take my medicine. My diabetes was close to being out of control. Was it too late to get myself back together again and lead a healthy life?

No. I know it's never too late. Just as the Lord guides me along the other paths of my life, he will guide me along the path of diabetes. He will give me the strength I need.

Prayer: Dear Father, help me to keep my diabetes under control, and when I mess up, guide me back to safety once again. Amen.

Sweet Talk 11

But when the time had fully come, God sent his Son,
born of a woman, born under law, that we might
receive the full rights of sons.

—Gal. 4:4-5 NIV

Tick tock. Time to measure my blood sugar.
Tick tock. Time to take my insulin shot.

It seems like the clock runs my day and my diabetes. I once recorded how long it took me to do each diabetes task during one twenty-four-hour period. When I added up the figures, I was amazed to find out I spent several hours each day just taking care of my diabetes.

I sometimes resent having to cram meal planning, the drawing up of insulin, monitoring, exercising, and taking other medicines into an already crowded schedule. But then I remember the time that you, dear Jesus, spent with us here on earth. You took time to come down from your eternal home in heaven to be with us. You took time to teach us, to lead us, and to die for us so that we may have eternal life.

I can't remember a single instance in Scripture in which you complained about the amount of time you spent away from your heavenly Father. Instead, you showed your all-encompassing love for us by allowing yourself to be nailed to a cross. Because you took the time away from your heavenly home, we can be with God for all eternity.

Prayer: Jesus, thank you for sacrificing yourself so that I can be reconciled to the Lord my God. And thank you, dear Lord, for helping me to find time each day to lead a healthy life. Amen.

Sweet Talk 12

As a mother comforts her child, so will I comfort you; and you will be comforted over Jerusalem.
—Isa. 66:13 NIV

Blah, blah, blah. Her lips are moving, but I'm not listening. I don't even want to be here, but I don't have much choice.

My doctor made me see his diabetes educator because I had some high readings. She's supposed to help me. How? Can she cure my diabetes? Don't think so.

I don't like anything about this disease. Not the finger pokes, not having to plan everything I eat, not having to exercise when I'd really rather sit on the couch.

Through the fog of my angry thoughts, I realize she's asking a question. She wants to know what bothers me most about my diabetes.

I explode and tell her everything bothers me. I tell her nothing's the same in my life any more. I tell her my life is run by diabetes. Then I start crying.

She gets up from her chair and hugs and comforts me. I feel her arms around me, and I lean on them. I know that she cares and really does want to help me live successfully with diabetes. Knowing that she cares about me is a wonderful feeling.

After I wipe away the cleansing tears, we work together on a strategy to help me cope with my anger and with daily life. I leave her with thanks and renewed strength to cope with diabetes.

Prayer: Dear Lord, I know you care about me, too, and I thank you for leading me to someone who could help me escape from my anger. Please help me to stay strong so I don't sink back into the mire of resentment. Amen.

Sweet Talk 13

The LORD will guide you always; he will satisfy your needs in a sun-scorched land and will strengthen your frame. You will be like a well-watered garden, like a spring whose waters never fail.
—Isa. 58:11 NIV

My diabetes tool kit is packed for the day. I marvel at the stuff I have to carry around. Meter, strips, lancets, medicines, logbook. I shake my head. I have an extra bag just for all this stuff. Then I realize how lucky I am to have these tools.

I know measuring blood sugar has come a long way since the days of urine testing. Now I can test my blood sugar directly with my meter. Since the days the first blood sugar monitor came on the market, sample sizes have gotten smaller, and monitors have gotten faster and more accurate. Also, medicines have been developed to control diabetes through various mechanisms. And more medications are on the way. Needles have gotten smaller, too.

Back in the days when insulin was first discovered, none of these management tools were available. Everything was guesswork. Now I have the means to control my diabetes.

I also have something else in my tool kit that makes daily life easier—your written Word, Lord. Without your Word guiding me, my daily life would be as difficult as trying to tell what my blood sugar is by looking at my finger.

With God's Word and my monitor, I find guidance for the new day.

Prayer: Thank you, Lord, for inspiring people to develop new ways for me to handle my diabetes more easily. Amen.

SUCCESSES

Sweet Talk 14

God saw all that he had made, and it was very good.

—Gen. 1:31a NIV

I'd been walking in the hills for about thirty minutes when I decided to take a break. I sat down on a rock and looked out over the valley.

Green grass, like the finest velvet, covered the hills. Tree branches sported leaves that were the bright yellow-green color of spring. Purple and orange wild flowers, awakened by the sun, brought splashes of color to the hills.

I felt the light breeze on my face. I closed my eyes and took a deep breath—breathing in the scent of new life, of new beginnings.

A red-tailed hawk flew over my head, floating on the air currents. His flight was effortless. Not so much as a wing flap. I wished I could see the world from his view—high above everything.

Then I realized that I had been high above everything for a few moments. I'd taken a brief vacation from diabetes and had forgotten all the tasks I needed to perform to care for myself. I'd been given a respite to enjoy God's creation and put things in perspective.

My rest stop showed me I could fit diabetes care into my life and enjoy my life all at the same time. Thank you, Lord.

Prayer: Lord, when diabetes care threatens to overwhelm me, please help me to remember the beautiful things in life, and the blessings you have given me. Amen.

Sweet Talk 15

He said to me, "My grace is sufficient for you, for my power is made perfect in weakness." Therefore I will boast all the more gladly about my weaknesses, so that Christ's power may rest on me.
——2 Cor. 12:9 NIV

When I was first diagnosed with diabetes, I wondered if that word was stamped on my forehead. I knew it was a label I'd be stuck with for the rest of my life. Would people treat me differently? How would it affect me, my family, and my job?

I prayed that the disease would be taken from me just as Paul prayed that the thorn in his flesh would be taken from him. Both of us got the same answer—the thorn would remain.

Like all thorns, sometimes diabetes is painful. Surprisingly, though, I've found blessings. I've learned to live healthier by making good food choices and exercising. I've treasured every moment with my family and tried to make the most of every day.

Also like Paul, I've realized that I can lean on Christ's strength and tell other people about how He's loved and cared for me by dying for me. That's what I want people to see impressed on my forehead—the sign of the cross.

Prayer: Dear Lord, please let my infirmity be a witness to the love you and your Son have for all men. And please let me feel your strength in my weakness. Amen.

Sweet Talk 16

I have fought the good fight, I have finished the race,
I have kept the faith.

—2 Tim. 4:7 NIV

Dear Lord, just like Paul, I finished a race today. It was a 5K fundraiser for diabetes, and I walked it, but the point is I participated.

When I first heard about the event, I was excited. We needed funds to get the word out about diabetes to the local community, and I thought I'd help by sponsoring a runner. But then the grandkids stepped in. They convinced me that their granddad could walk that race and make a difference by doing it.

I started training, and you were with me, literally, every step of the way, Lord. When I started training, I started slow and built up my muscles and endurance.

On the day of the race I made sure my blood sugar stayed in range and carried my fast-acting carb. I felt your presence, Father, in the breeze, the sunshine, and at the rest points.

As I neared the finish line, I saw my family pointing at me and urging me on. After I finished, I got big hugs from everyone. My grandchildren were so proud, and so was I. Lord, you helped me keep the faith.

Prayer: Father, thank you for helping me through the race of life and for showing me once again that you are always present. Amen.

Sweet Talk 17

*Because you are my help, I sing in the shadow of
your wings. My soul clings to you; your right hand
upholds me.*

—Ps. 63:7-8 NIV

I practically skipped out of the doctor's office today.
My A1C was 6.5, and my logbook confirmed my
blood sugar levels were where they should be. I'd
been following my diet and exercise plan and the
medicines were doing their job.

Time to celebrate! I deserved a gigantic pat on
the back. As I got in the car, I thought of different
possibilities for rewarding myself. In the old days, I
would have gone to the ice cream parlor and ordered
up a big hot fudge sundae. Not a good idea now.

Most celebrations, I realized, are centered
on food. As children, many of us were rewarded

with a treat of some kind—the higher the calorie count, the better. I'd have to break out of that mold somehow.

I sat in the car thinking. What did I like to do besides eat? I liked to read. I liked movies. I liked good music. I began to realize there were lots of ways to reward myself besides scarfing down a brownie.

There was one place that held the answer to my celebration dilemma—the mall. I pulled up to the music store and purchased a CD I'd been wanting to buy. I popped it in the car player and headed home—the beautiful music was my reward for having a good day at the doctor's office.

Prayer: Lord, thank you for helping me to see other possibilities for rewards in my life, and for helping me solve a problem. Amen.

SWEET TALK 18

Listen to advice and accept instruction, and in the end you will be wise.

—Prov. 19:20 NIV

There was a time when I didn't believe I had diabetes.

Even when my doctor told me my blood sugar was over 300; I didn't feel any different. No one could tell by looking at me that I had a chronic disease, so it was easy to pretend I didn't.

I went on leading my life as I had in the past—not worrying about diet or taking any other action that might contribute to improving my health. Then I started noticing things. My energy level dropped, but I attributed that to the fact that I had to get up and go to the bathroom several times a night. My vision wasn't as sharp as it used to be. I put that down to the fact that maybe I needed new glasses. When my feet started tingling, though, I knew I had to do something.

I went back to the doctor, became educated about diabetes, and then got serious about treating it.

I feel better now that I have accepted the fact that I have a chronic disease.

Prayer: Dear Lord, please give me the strength to continue to accept the fact that I have diabetes and please give me the strength to live accordingly. Amen.

Sweet Talk 19

His divine power has given us everything we need
for life and godliness through our knowledge of him
who called us by his own glory and goodness.
—2 Pet. 1:3 NIV

I recently saw a film about an old sailing vessel and its adventurous captain. The captain reminded me that I am the captain of my diabetes.

Sure, I've had education about diabetes, and I've learned to use the gadgets associated with diabetes management. So far, though, I haven't been able to persuade anyone to come by and cook my meals or run home lab tests to see how my glucose levels are doing.

Those jobs are mine and mine alone.

Most of the time I like being in control of my diabetes, but sometimes I feel overwhelmed and wish I could get out from under all the daily tasks I have to perform just to stay healthy.

Then I remember that you, Lord, are my loving Captain. You will always be there to see me through the hard patches of life. You will always be there to hear my daily prayers. You will always give me the strength I ask for and need.

With you at my side, Lord, I will be able to steer a straight course through diabetes.

Prayer: Father, thank you for always being there, for always being a font of blessings and a source of strength for me. Please help me to remember the blessings you have bestowed upon me. Amen.

Sweet Talk 20

Thanks be to God for his indescribable gift!
—2 Cor. 9:15 NIV

"Thank you."

I smile at the ophthalmologist as I put my glasses back on. He's just examined my eyes and says everything looks great.

As I leave his office, I think about all the other people I say thank you to for my diabetes care—my family physician who checks me every three months, my endocrinologist who fine-tunes my care, my podiatrist who checks my feet, my dentist who makes sure my teeth and gums are fine, and my educator who explains my diabetes to me in terms I can understand.

Thank you is such a simple, yet meaningful phrase.

Then I think about you, Jesus, my precious Savior.

No one thanked you while you were hanging on the cross after being scourged and beaten. No one thanked you as you said, "Father, forgive them for they know not what they do." No one thanked you as your life's blood poured out from the wound in your side, and you gave yourself as a sacrifice for us all.

I can't imagine what went through your mind as you hung on that cross, but I thank you daily for the greatest sacrifice the world has ever known. And I am humbled knowing that you willingly sacrificed yourself for me.

Prayer: Dear Jesus, thank you for paying the price for me and for all mankind. I pray that you never let me forget the forgiveness you bought for me. Amen.

TREATMENT

Sweet Talk 21

But those who hope in the LORD *will renew their strength. They will soar on wings like eagles; they will run and not grow weary, they will walk and not be faint.*

—Isa. 40:31 NIV

I groaned when I first found out I'd have to find time to work out. I'm not the leotard-sweatband type. But, I decided that if exercise would help, then I'd do it.

For a while I felt like a martyr taking time out of my day to ride my stationary bike. Same routine every day. Boring! Then I started looking around for other possibilities.

I found that doing the same bike ride at the gym wasn't boring because it allowed me to talk to people. Water aerobics was fun because I felt weightless—a feeling I hadn't experienced in years. And square dance class was one of my best finds. Moving to music didn't seem like exercise at all.

Even a walk in the neighborhood was a treasured opportunity. I could watch the seasons change and catch up on how my neighbors were doing.

I suppose I'll have to wait until I get to heaven to run and not grow weary, but I'm thankful for all the fun opportunities the Lord has given me to help me care for my diabetes.

Prayer: Lord, thank you for opening my eyes to all the ways I can control my blood sugar while still having fun. Amen.

Sweet Talk 22

Turn your ear to me, come quickly to my rescue;
be my rock of refuge, a strong fortress to save me.
Since you are my rock and my fortress, for the sake
of your name lead and guide me.

—Ps. 31:2-3 NIV

My doctor started me on a new pill for my diabetes today. I was already taking one medicine for it and couldn't understand why I'd have to take another one. Did I fail at something? I'd tried to eat right and exercise; tried to lower the stress in my life. What more could I do?

I took the prescription to the pharmacist and talked to her about it. She said there was more than one way to lower blood sugar. Apparently, some medicines help the pancreas release insulin, others shut off glucose from coming out of the liver, and still others slow down carb absorption or help glucose get into muscle cells. She said my doctor must really be paying attention to my diabetes, since he ordered another type of pill to help my body have closer to normal blood sugars.

When I left the pharmacy, I was calmer. It was good to know that I had people watching over me, just as you are always watching over me, Lord.

Prayer: Lord, thank you for guiding all the people who help me with diabetes. Please give them the strength to continue to help people like me. Amen.

SWEET TALK 23

Trust in the LORD forever, for the LORD, the LORD, is the Rock eternal.

—Isa. 26:4 NIV

I have to start on insulin. I thought I'd done something wrong, but the doctor said no. He said the cells in my pancreas that made insulin had gradually lost their function over time. I've taken every pill on the market for diabetes, trying to avoid this day, but it's here now.

The nurse showed me how to inject insulin into my stomach. I was surprised when it didn't hurt at all. She watched me to make sure I did everything right. But this is all so new to me, Lord. Will I have the skills I need to do this thing? Will I be able to cope with this change in my life? What will strangers think when I pull a syringe out? Will they think I'm some kind of drug addict?

Yet, as I ask, I know you will be by my side as I start this new phase in my life. You will be there to guide me as I make decisions and learn new skills. And how do I know that? Because you have promised you will never leave or forsake me.

Prayer: Lord, change is hard. Please help me through this time of learning so I can make the transition to better diabetes control. Amen.

Sweet Talk 24

So he got up from the meal, took off his outer clothing, and wrapped a towel around his waist. After that, he poured water into a basin and began to wash his disciples' feet, drying them with a towel that was wrapped around him.

—John 13:4-5 NIV

In his heart a man plans his course, but the LORD determines his steps.

—Prov. 16:9 NIV

My feet like this time of day—the time when I apply lotion and inspect what the kids call my piggy toes. The lotion feels good as I rub it in. It makes my feet soft and it prevents the skin from cracking. I carefully examine my feet as I apply the lotion.

No red spots, blisters, or cuts. Good.

As I put on my shoes and socks, I think back to the time when Jesus walked on this earth. His feet felt the same soft grass and hard stones ours do. He walked the same life that we do now.

At the Last Supper he took the role of servant and washed the disciples' feet. His followers didn't realize it, but he would go on to perform the greatest act of service to all mankind. He would die for our sins.

Now we can walk in the Lord's favor, forgiven of our sins. Now we can step out and spread the message of God's love to everyone.

Prayer: Dear Lord, thank you for sending your Son to us that we may have everlasting life. Let our feet be swift and sure as they carry your love to all. Amen.

SWEET TALK 25

Those who know your name will trust in you, for you, LORD, have never forsaken those who seek you.

—Ps. 9:10 NIV

Lord, I'm apprehensive. The trainer's coming tomorrow to start me on an insulin pump, and I'm not sure how it will affect my life. I've been practicing with the pump and getting more skilled at using it, but tomorrow it will be attached to my body. I'm wondering how it will feel to wear something all the time. I'm wondering if the pump will interfere with my daily activities.

Of course, you know I don't have much choice. I've been on a roller coaster of highs and lows for months even though I've been careful. The lows at night especially scare me. My spouse doesn't even sleep any more—afraid that I'll go low and not wake up.

The pump is supposed to deliver insulin in a more dependable manner. I sure hope so. I do know that you are always dependable. You are always with me in the highs and lows of life. I know you will see me through this latest challenge.

Prayer: Thank you, Lord, for never forsaking me—for always being there when I need you. Your strength and love are truly awesome. Amen.

Sweet Talk 26

But thanks be to God! He gives us the victory through our LORD Jesus Christ.
—1 Cor. 15:57 NIV

Why was I ever afraid to use an insulin pump? I feel like a pro now and am starting to use the extra features the trainer showed me. I'm using less insulin, and I'm off the highs and lows roller coaster. Meals are a breeze. I count the carbs, punch in the insulin dose, and the pump does the rest.

I've become so used to the pump that it seems like it's always been part of my life. I couldn't stand being without it. Just as I couldn't stand being without you, Lord. You gave me victory over sin and death by the gift of your Son, Jesus Christ. You gave me victory over my fears and led me along the way to learning a new skill.

Help me to remember this triumph when I'm feeling discouraged. Help me to feel your loving arms around me when diabetes closes in on me. Help me to appreciate the love my family gives me daily.

Prayer: Lord, thank you for the victories you give us every day. Thank you, too, for the gift of your son, our Savior, Jesus Christ. Amen.

FOR RELATIVES OF
PEOPLE WITH
DIABETES

Sweet Talk 27

What can I do, Lord? My wife says she's tired of taking care of her diabetes. She says she's burned out. I can see her point. It's not fun to have to take time to measure blood sugars and figure out what you're going to eat. I know that, but I also know I love her and worry about what might happen to her.

She says she doesn't feel any different, but I know she's been getting up to go to the bathroom at night, just like she did before she was diagnosed.

She must be running high. I can feel myself getting angry because of what she's doing to me and to the family. We're all worried.

How do I get through to her without sounding preachy? How do I make her understand how important she is to us? How do I convince her that a little extra care now may prevent bigger problems in the future?

Prayer: Lord, please give me the words to talk to ____. I want ____ to understand how important he or she is to me. Help me to convey my love and concern. Lord, I know you care more than anyone, and you will lead me. Amen.

Sweet Talk 28

And now these three remain: faith, hope, and love.
But the greatest of these is love.
—1 Cor. 13:13 NIV

Lord, I have waited on your guidance, and today it paid off. You know I've been worried about ____. He hasn't been taking care of himself the way he should. The whole family's been concerned. I've wanted to talk to him about our worries, but how could I approach him without seeming to be self-righteous or angry about his behavior?

You gave me a plan. I waited for a day when neither of us had any activities, and the grandparents could take the kids. It was quiet in the house. We could talk with each other without being interrupted.

After lunch, I took his hands in mine and told him how much I loved him. Then in calm tones, I told him how worried I was about him. How I didn't want to judge him or make him feel guilty—only that I wanted him to know what my feelings were and how much I cared.

We both shed a few tears. And how could we do anything other than bring our concerns before your throne?

Prayer: Lord, we come before you today because we know you have perfect love for us. We ask for strength to deal with diabetes and for understanding when sometimes diabetes control isn't perfect. We thank you for giving us each other. We ask for your guidance in our lives. Amen.

Sweet Talk 29

Let us come before him with thanksgiving and extol him with music and song.

—Ps. 95:2 NIV

The grocery list on my desk nagged at me to write something on it. I tapped my pencil on the desk and scratched my head—all to no avail. No inspired food ideas popped into my head. What to do?

A relative was going to spend his first Thanksgiving away from home with us. We were looking forward to his visit; but he had diabetes, and I hadn't a clue as to what to feed him.

I didn't want to offend him by serving something he shouldn't eat. I also didn't want to make him feel uncomfortable by preparing him a different meal from the rest of the guests. Could I serve the traditional menu everyone had come to expect and still make my nephew feel welcome?

A phone call to his mother answered all my questions. She said turkey was a perfect main dish. She also gave me hints on how to cut down on fats and calories in other recipes by using no-calorie sweeteners, cooking spray, and low-fat ingredients.

As I scribbled away at my grocery list, I realized we would all benefit from my nephew's visit because we would be eating a healthy and delicious Thanksgiving dinner.

Prayer: Dear Father, thank you for giving me the resources to show my nephew how much I love him. Also please watch over him and keep him in good health. Amen.

PREGNANCY

Sweet Talk 30

*May he give you the desire of your heart and make
all your plans succeed.*

—Ps. 20:4 NIV

So many things to be done. I ticked off the list of
tasks while I waited for the results of my test.
Finish getting the baby's room decorated and pick
up the crib. Get Mom's room ready so she's comfort-
able while she's helping me with the baby. Get a bag
out so I can start thinking what about to pack for
the trip to the hospital.

I was still scratching notes when the doctor came
in the room and opened my chart. He told me the test
results showed I had something called *gestational
diabetes*. He explained that my blood sugar level
was high and that I'd have to see a dietitian about
planning my meals. I'd have to start measuring my

blood with some kind of monitor. To top that off, he told me that if my blood sugar wasn't controlled by diet and exercise, then I might have to start taking insulin. He said if I didn't do these things, my baby and I could have real problems when I gave birth.

The words spun in my head as the doctor spoke: *diabetes, monitor, diet, insulin.* I clasped my abdomen, wanting to protect my baby from these words. What would this new challenge mean to my unborn child? During the drive home, I wondered how I was going to handle this new situation—how I could protect my baby. Then I felt your presence, Lord, and I knew. I knew you would help me through this pregnancy.

Prayer: Lord, please give me the strength to do everything I need to do to deliver a healthy baby. And, Lord, please let us raise that child in your ways so that he knows the love you have for him. Amen.

SWEET TALK 31

I will praise you forever for what you have done; in your name I will hope, for your name is good. I will praise you in the presence of your saints.

—Ps. 52:9 NIV

Your word is a lamp to my feet and a light for my path.

—Ps. 119:105 NIV

Lord, thank you, thank you, thank you. As I hold my newborn son in my arms, I give praise and thanks to you.

You knew the road through pregnancy and birth would be a little harder for me than other women since I have diabetes. Because of that rocky path, you sent helpers to me to see me through.

As my husband and I planned for our baby, we sought help and found out that good control would be important even before I got pregnant. You led me through that opening gate to the road of motherhood. You guided me around the bends of morning sickness and increased insulin use as my pregnancy progressed. You gave me strength to do moderate exercise and to stick to my plan. And during that last long, hard month, you gave my husband extra patience.

In the delivery room, we clasped each other's hands as we heard our healthy baby's first cry. Now as I look at my baby's face in the quiet of my hospital room, my child and I say our first prayer to you. Lord, thank you for a safe pregnancy. Thank you for life. And thank you for the many blessings you bring into our lives that we never even see or acknowledge.

Prayer: Lord, thank you for being at my side all through this pregnancy. Thank you for the blessing of a healthy baby and the opportunity to bring a new life to you. Amen.

MONTHLY GOALS

JANUARY

God is our refuge and strength, an ever-present help in trouble.

—Ps. 46:1 NIV

My goal this month is:

_____

_____

_____

The first step I will take to meet this goal is:

_____

_____

_____

FEBRUARY

When I called, you answered me; you made me bold and stouthearted.

—Ps. 138:3 NIV

My goal this month is:

_____

_____

_____

The first step I will take to meet this goal is:

_____

_____

_____

MARCH

And we rejoice in the hope of the glory of God. Not only so, but we also rejoice in our sufferings, because we know that suffering produces perseverance; perseverance, character; and character, hope.
—Rom. 5:2b-4 NIV

My goal this month is:

_____

_____

_____

The first step I will take to meet this goal is:

_____

_____

_____

APRIL

Jesus said to her, "I am the resurrection and the life. He who believes in me will live, even though he dies; and whoever lives and believes in me will never die."

—John 11:25-26 NIV

My goal this month is:

_____

_____

_____

The first step I will take to meet this goal is:

_____

_____

_____

MAY

Be very careful, then, how you live—not as unwise but as wise, making the most of every opportunity.

—Eph. 5:15-16a NIV

My goal this month is:

_____

_____

_____

The first step I will take to meet this goal is:

_____

_____

_____

JUNE

Blessed is the man who trusts in the LORD, *whose confidence is in him.*

—Jer. 17:7 NIV

My goal this month is:

_____

_____

_____

The first step I will take to meet this goal is:

_____

_____

_____

July

*From the fullness of his grace we have all received
one blessing after another.*

—John 1:16 NIV

My goal this month is:

_____

_____

_____

The first step I will take to meet this goal is:

_____

_____

_____

AUGUST

"I will be a Father to you, and you will be my sons and daughters," says the Lord Almighty.
—2 Cor. 6:18 NIV

My goal this month is:

_____

_____

_____

The first step I will take to meet this goal is:

_____

_____

_____

SEPTEMBER

My eyes are fixed on you, O Sovereign LORD; in you I take refuge.

—Ps. 141:8 NIV

My goal this month is:

_____

_____

_____

The first step I will take to meet this goal is:

_____

_____

_____

OCTOBER

For the LORD is good and his love endures forever; his faithfulness continues through all generations.
—Ps. 100:5 NIV

My goal this month is:

_____

_____

_____

The first step I will take to meet this goal is:

_____

_____

_____

NOVEMBER

Let them give thanks to the LORD *for his unfailing love and his wonderful deeds for men, for he satisfies the thirsty and fills the hungry with good things.*
—Ps. 107:8-9 NIV

My goal this month is:

_____

_____

_____

The first step I will take to meet this goal is:

_____

_____

_____

DECEMBER

For to us a child is born, to us a son is given, and the government will be on his shoulders. And he will be called Wonderful Counselor, Mighty God, Everlasting Father, Prince of Peace.

—Isa. 9:6 NIV

My goal this month is:

_____

_____

_____

The first step I will take to meet this goal is:

_____

_____

_____

Blood Glucose
Logs

Day	Break-fast	Lunch	Dinner	Bed-time	Other/Snack	Com-ments
	Pre Carbs	Pre Carbs	Pre Carbs	Carbs	Carbs	Diet, exercise,
	Post Insulin	Post Insulin	Post Insulin	Insulin	Insulin	Illness, stress
M						
	/	/	/	/	/	
Tu						
	/	/	/	/	/	
W						
	/	/	/	/	/	
Th						
	/	/	/	/	/	
F						
	/	/	/	/	/	
Sa						
	/	/	/	/	/	
Su						
	/	/	/	/	/	

To help you detect patterns: Highlight high readings and circle low readings in red.

What you heard from me, keep as a pattern of sound teaching, with faith and love in Christ Jesus.
—2 Tim. 1:13 NIV

Day	Break-fast	Lunch	Dinner	Bed-time	Other/Snack	Com-ments
	Pre Carbs	Pre Carbs	Pre Carbs	Carbs	Carbs	Diet, exercise,
	Post Insulin	Post Insulin	Post Insulin	Insulin	Insulin	Illness, stress
M						
	/	/	/	/	/	
Tu						
	/	/	/	/	/	
W						
	/	/	/	/	/	
Th						
	/	/	/	/	/	
F						
	/	/	/	/	/	
Sa						
	/	/	/	/	/	
Su						
	/	/	/	/	/	

To help you detect patterns: Note if you had a high or low blood sugar at the same time for three days in a row.

"I am able to destroy the temple of God and rebuild it in three days."

—Matt. 26:61b NIV

Day	Break-fast	Lunch	Dinner	Bed-time	Other/ Snack	Com-ments
	Pre Carbs	Pre Carbs	Pre Carbs	Carbs	Carbs	Diet, exercise,
	Post Insulin	Post Insulin	Post Insulin	Insulin	Insulin	Illness, stress
M						
	/	/	/	/	/	
Tu						
	/	/	/	/	/	
W						
	/	/	/	/	/	
Th						
	/	/	/	/	/	
F						
	/	/	/	/	/	
Sa						
	/	/	/	/	/	
Su						
	/	/	/	/	/	

If you have a high or low blood sugar, be sure to write down the reason you think the event occurred.

Prepare your minds for action; be self-controlled; set your hope fully on the grace to be given you when Jesus Christ is revealed.

—1 Pet. 1:13 NIV

Day	Break-fast	Lunch	Dinner	Bed-time	Other/ Snack	Com-ments
	Pre Carbs	Pre Carbs	Pre Carbs	Carbs	Carbs	Diet, exercise,
	Post Insulin	Post Insulin	Post Insulin	Insulin	Insulin	Illness, stress
M						
	/	/	/	/	/	
Tu						
	/	/	/	/	/	
W						
	/	/	/	/	/	
Th						
	/	/	/	/	/	
F						
	/	/	/	/	/	
Sa						
	/	/	/	/	/	
Su						
	/	/	/	/	/	

Please remember that your blood glucose monitor is an informational tool to guide you through the path of diabetes.

The path of life leads upward for the wise to keep him from going down to the grave.
—Prov. 15:24 NIV

Racing for the Prize
Exercise Troubleshooting

Do you not know that in a race all the runners run,
but only one gets the prize? Run in such a way as
to get the prize.

—1 Cor. 9:24 NIV

Prayer: Lord, I know how valuable exercise is to my
diabetes control, but sometimes I get tired
of doing the same old thing. Sometimes
I'd rather just sit. Please help me think of
ways to incorporate more movement into
my daily life. In Jesus' name, Amen.

Activities that would be fun to do:

_____

_____

_____

_____

Activities I wouldn't get tired of doing:

_____

_____

_____

_____

BREAD OF LIFE
FOOD TROUBLESHOOTING

Meanwhile his disciples urged him, "Rabbi, eat something." But he said to them, "I have food to eat that you know nothing about." ... "My food," said Jesus, "is to do the will of him who sent me and to finish his work."

—John 4:31-32, 34 NIV

Prayer: Dear Father, I know food is as important as medicine in the treatment of my diabetes. Please help and guide me and those folks assisting me with my food plan to come up with menus I will enjoy eating. In Jesus' name, Amen.

Foods I enjoy eating:

_____   _____

_____   _____

_____   _____

_____   _____

_____   _____

SCRIPTURE
REFERENCES

**Scriptures used in
devotional:**

Isaiah 43:2-3
Proverbs 4:11
1 Corinthians 10:13
Genesis 1:31a
Isaiah 40:31
Proverbs 22:6 &
Psalm 68:19
2 Corinthians 12:9
Psalm 111:5 &
Psalm 121:2
Isaiah 41:13
Psalm 48:14
2 Corinthians 1:3-4

2 Timothy 4:7
Psalm 31:2-3
Isaiah 26:4
Psalm 63:7-8
Proverbs 16:3
John 13:4-5 &
Proverbs 16:9
1 Corinthians 1:18
Psalm 9:10
1 Corinthians 15:57
Psalm 16:11
Psalm 20:4
1 Corinthians 13:13
Psalm 52:9 &
Psalm 119:105
Galatians 4:4-5

Isaiah 66:13
Isaiah 58:11
Proverbs 19:20
Psalm 95:2
2 Peter 1:3
2 Corinthians 9:15
Philemon 4:1

Goals Scriptures:
Psalm 46:1
Psalm 138:3
Romans 5:2b-4
John 11:25-26
Ephesians 5:15-16a
Jeremiah 17:7
John 1:16
2 Corinthians 6:18

Psalm 141:8
Psalm 100:5
Psalm 107:8-9
Isaiah 9:6

Log Scriptures:
2 Timothy 1:13
Matthew 26-61b
1 Peter 1:13
Proverbs 15:24

Racing for the Prize
1 Corinthians 9:24

Food Troubleshooting
John 4:21-32, 34

Printed in the United States
144365LV00001B/44/P